PIANO FOR BEGINNERS
LEARN TO PLAY
NURSERY RHYMES

THE ULTIMATE BEGINNER PIANO SONGBOOK
FOR KIDS WITH LESSONS ON READING NOTES
AND 50 BELOVED SONGS

Producer & International Distributor
eBookPro Publishing
www.ebook-pro.com

Piano for Beginners
Piano Made Easy Press

Transcribed by Seyapianist
ISBN: 9798827286271

Contact: agency@ebook-pro.com

CONTENTS

INTRODUCTION

Welcome to your child's first piano book!

Whether your kid has been begging to learn for years, is just picking up a new hobby, or you simply acquired this book to encourage a love of music in your child, these pages hold everything you will need to get started.

With 50 beloved and well-known nursery rhymes accompanied by an introductory lesson on the basics of reading notes and divided into three difficulty levels with music lessons throughout, your child can learn to play the piano with no further instruction required.

All they will need in addition to this book is a piano or keyboard and some time to practice. Remember – practice makes perfect, and the wide range of songs in this collection will make practicing a true pleasure.

HOW TO USE THIS BOOK

First, read the Get to Know Your Piano section on pages 10-14 with your child.

This short guide will teach you and them the fundamentals of reading notes, after which, and with a little practice, any beginning musician will be able to read and play all the music in Level 1 of this book.

Once your child has practiced the songs in Level 1 and feels comfortable learning something new, go on to the second lesson on page 32. This will teach you and them some new things that will allow them to play all the Level 2 songs in the book, which are slightly more complex.

Once you've perfected Level 2 and want to learn something more, open up lesson three on page 52. Here, you will find yet more neat tips and tricks to advance your child's playing skills and open up the next and final level in this book – Level 3.

Don't forget, you can always go back and play earlier songs, even if you've already learned more advanced ones!

As this is meant to be a First Piano Book, all the songs can be played with one hand. For more advanced learners, we have included chords that can be played with the left hand as well, simultaneously. You will find an explanation for playing chords in Level 3.

SPECIAL VIDEO / AUDIO FEATURE

Learning from a book can be challenging – and sometimes audio and visual aids can help. That is why we've included a special feature in this beginner piano book.

You will notice that every piece of music is accompanied by a QR code adjacent to the title.

Scan the QR code to access a video of that very song being played on piano, where you can hear exactly what the music should sound like and see precisely how to play each note.

Slow the video down or speed it up, skip forward and pause at your convenience – whatever helps you master the tune.

Level 1

GET TO KNOW YOUR PIANO

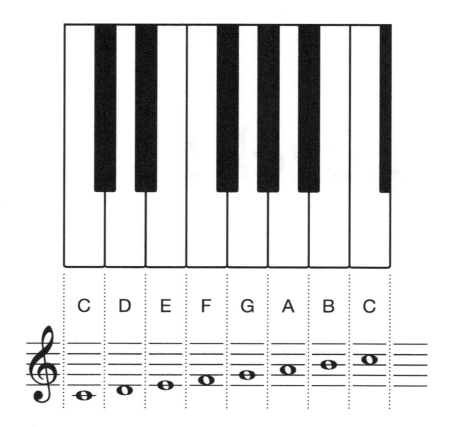

RECOGNIZING KEYS

A piano is made up of **keys**, each of which makes a different sound – called a **note**.

A piano has white keys and black keys – we call the white ones by their letters, from A-G – just like you can see in the picture.

You will notice that the black keys come in groups – first two, then three, and so on.

Look at your piano – and put your finger on the C note. You will recognize it as the white key immediately on the left of the group of two black keys. You will notice that there are several different C keys on your keyboard – we'll always start with the one closest to the middle.

From there, going to your right, play each white note, one at a time – C, D, E, F, G, A, B – just like in the picture.

The more you practice, the easier it will be to recognize the notes – but for now, just remember where the C key is, and work from there!

READING MUSIC

Now, look at the five lines with the swirly symbol on the left. This is a **Treble Clef** which indicates the beginning of a new line of music.

Musical notes are drawn on and between the lines, going from left to right, and now we will learn how to recognize them.

Find the C note on your piano again like we learned and look at how it looks on the lines. It is the only note with a line through it – and that is how we will remember it.

From there, the notes go higher up along the lines – with every consecutive note going up one half-line.

So after C comes D, which sits just below the first line. Next is E, which sits right on the middle of the first line – and so on.

The first few times you play, look back at the drawing to remind yourself which note goes where. Once you've practiced a few songs, you should remember them by heart more easily.

UNDERSTANDING NOTE LENGTHS

You will notice that some music notes are black, others are white, some have lines and some only ovals, and others are connected together with beams. All of these things help us understand how long we should keep our finger on the note before we go on to the next one.

This is a **quarter note**. It is the most common and the simplest. Put your finger on one of the piano keys and play a short note – count in your head or out loud to one, and then let go.

This is a **half note**. This note is **twice as long** as a regular note. This time, count to 2 before you let go.

This note is **even longer**, and you'll usually find it at the end of a line or song. It is called a **whole note**. Count to 4 before you move on to the next one.

This note is an 8th note – it is only **half as long** as a quarter note. Press the key once and don't hold your finger on it for long.

Whenever you see a dotted note, like these:

That means you must play for slightly longer than the regular length of the note. So, for example, a dotted quarter note (black with a straight line) will be played slightly longer than a regular quarter note, but less long than a half note.

When you see notes connected with a **beam**, like this:

That means you have to play the notes quickly, one after the other, without pausing in between.

You'll notice that each song has the lyrics written underneath, telling you exactly what to sing for every note.

So, you can also use your knowledge of the songs in the book to help you understand how long each note should be.

You'll notice that there are some capital letters above the music lines. These letters tell us what we should play with our left hand — and they are called chords. You can play all the songs in this book with your right hand only, or with both hands — this is a more advanced skill.

When you feel like you've mastered playing with your right hand, head over to Appendix A at the end of this book where you will find instructions on playing chords with your left hand.

GETTING STARTED

Let's look at this example of the first line of Baa Baa Black Sheep:

The numbers above the notes help show you which finger of your right hand to use when playing each note.

1 means use your thumb — and so on until 5, which is your pinky.

So in this example, you'd start with playing C twice with your thumb (remember, we read notes from left to right just like we read English), then G twice with your second finger, then A with your third, B with your fourth, C with your fifth, back again to A with your third and finally G with your second finger.

Try it — and sing along!

Remember, playing with the correct fingers is important and will help make sure you are playing the piano in the best possible way!

Congratulations! You've learned how to read music notes.
Now pick out a song and use what you've learned to make some beautiful music!

Rain, Rain, Go Away

Children's Nursery Rhyme

Rain, rain, go a-way, come a-gain a – no-ther day.

Lit – tle chil-dren want to play, rain – rain – go a-way.

Soft Kitty

Traditional Nursery Rhyme

Soft kit – ty, warm kit – ty, lit – tle ball of fur.

Hap-py kit – ty, slee-py kit – ty, purr, purr, purr.

16

Yankee Doodle

Traditional Nursery Rhyme

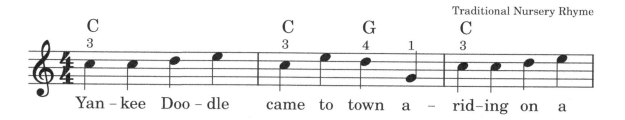

Yan – kee Doo – dle came to town a – rid-ing on a

po – ny. He stuck a fea-ther in his cap and called it ma-ca –

ro – ni.

Mary Had A Little Lamb

Children's Nursery Rhymes

Ma – ry had a lit – tle lamb, lit – tle lamb,
Ev' – ry – where that Ma – ry went, Ma – ry went,

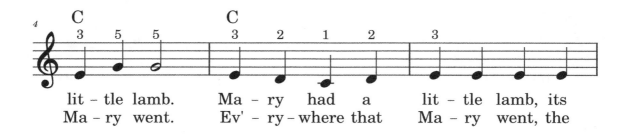

lit – tle lamb. Ma – ry had a lit – tle lamb, its
Ma – ry went. Ev' – ry – where that Ma – ry went, the

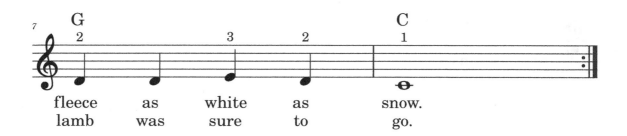

fleece as white as snow.
lamb was sure to go.

Au Clair De La Lune

French Folk Song

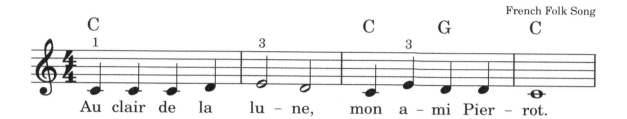

Hush-a-bye

Traditional Lullaby

Hush – a – bye, baby, on the tree – top.

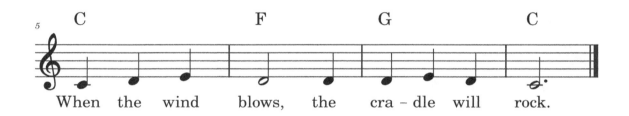

When the wind blows, the cra – dle will rock.

Ring Around A Rosie

Traditional Nursery Rhyme

Ring a–round a Ro – sie, a poc–ket full of po – sies.

A – shes, a – shes, we all fall down!

Polly Put The Kettle On

Traditional Nursery Rhyme

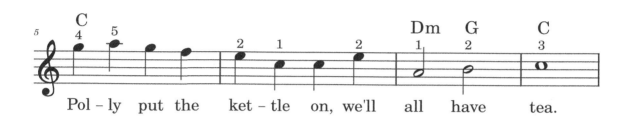

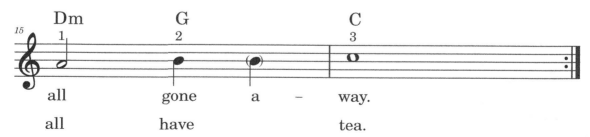

Merrily We Roll Along

Traditional

♩ = 120

Straight quarter note rhythm

Mer-ri-ly we roll a-long, roll a-long, roll a-long!

Mer-ri-ly we roll a-long a - cross the deep blue sea.

Dotted quarter note rhythm

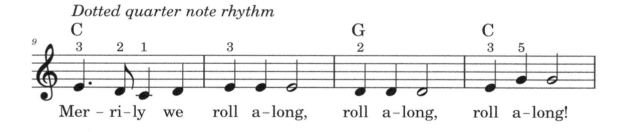

Mer-ri-ly we roll a-long, roll a-long, roll a-long!

Mer-ri-ly we roll a-long a - cross the deep blue sea.

Jack and Jill

Traditional Nursery Rhyme

Jack and Jill went up the hill to fetch a pail of wa – ter.

Jack fell down and broke his crown, and Jill came tum – bling af – ter.

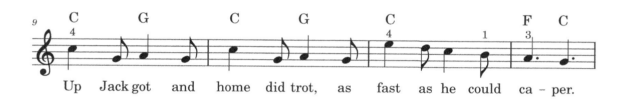

Up Jack got and home did trot, as fast as he could ca – per.

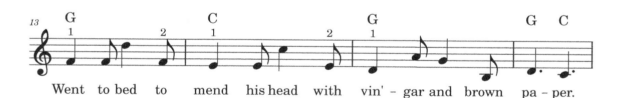

Went to bed to mend his head with vin' – gar and brown pa – per.

Jill came in and she did grin to see his pa – per plas – ter

Mo – ther vexed, did whip her next, for cau – sing Jack's di – sas – ter.

Ode To Joy

Ludwig van Beethoven

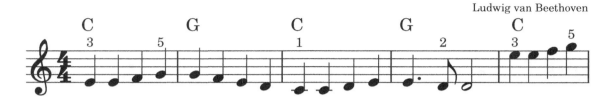

London Bridge

English Nursery Rhyme

 The Alphabet Song

Traditional Nursery Rhyme

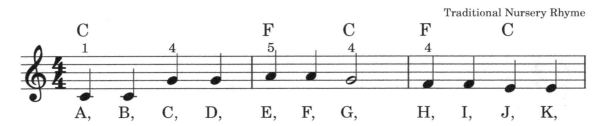

A, B, C, D, E, F, G, H, I, J, K,

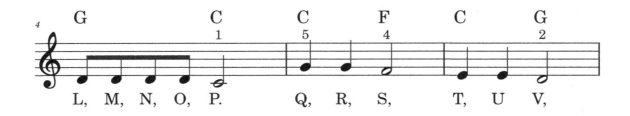

L, M, N, O, P. Q, R, S, T, U V,

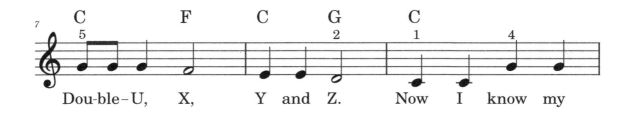

Dou-ble-U, X, Y and Z. Now I know my

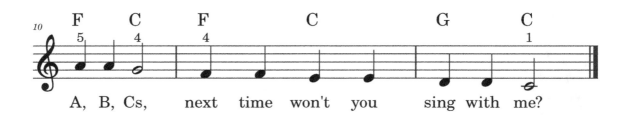

A, B, Cs, next time won't you sing with me?

Hot Cross Buns

Traditional

Hot cross buns, hot cross buns!

One a pen – ny, two a pen – ny, hot cross buns!

If you have no daugh – ters, give them to your sons.

One a pen – ny, two a pen – ny, hot cross buns!

Baa, Baa, Black Sheep

Children's Nursery Rhyme

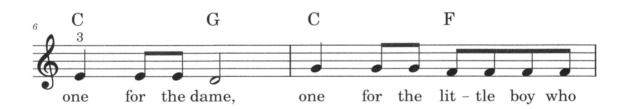

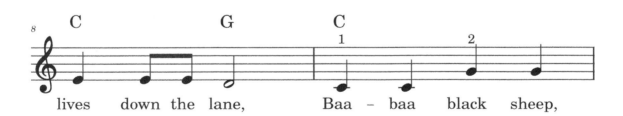

Five Little Monkeys

Children's Nursery Rhyme

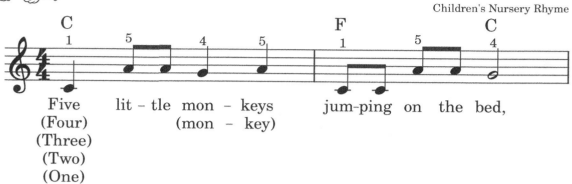

Five lit – tle mon – keys jum-ping on the bed,
(Four) (mon – key)
(Three)
(Two)
(One)

one fell down and bumped his head. So

Mom – my called the doc – tor and the doc – tor said:

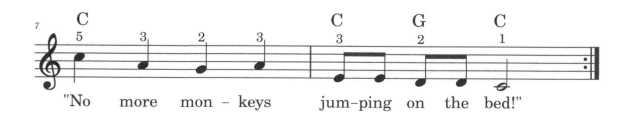

"No more mon – keys jum-ping on the bed!"

29

Twinkle Twinkle Little Star

French Folk Tune and Children's Song

Level 2

RESTS

This symbol is a rest:

It means take a break, and count in your head to one before you play the next note. It is the same length as a quarter note.

SHARPS AND FLATS

The black keys on the piano are called *sharps* or *flats*, and they don't have their own names. **D sharp** means the black key to the **right** of D. **D flat** means the black key to the left of D.

A sharp is recognized by this symbol:

While a flat is recognized by this one:

So whenever you see one of these symbols on the music lines next to a note, you'll play the black key that is immediately next to that note – on its right if it is sharp ♯ or its left if it is flat ♭.

Sometimes, throughout the entire song one or two notes will always be sharps or flats. So, instead of putting a sharp or flat symbol next to every single note, we'll put the symbol once at the beginning of every line of music, right next to the Treble Clef, like this:

This is called a **Key Signature.**

In this example, whenever there is a B in the song, we'll make sure to play B flat – the black key immediately to the left of B.

Sometimes, we can have more than one sharp or flat in the song:

In this example, we can see that whenever there is a C or F in the song, we'll play C# or F# - in other words, the black key to the right of C or the black key to the right of F, accordingly.

Five Little Ducks

Children's Nursery Rhyme

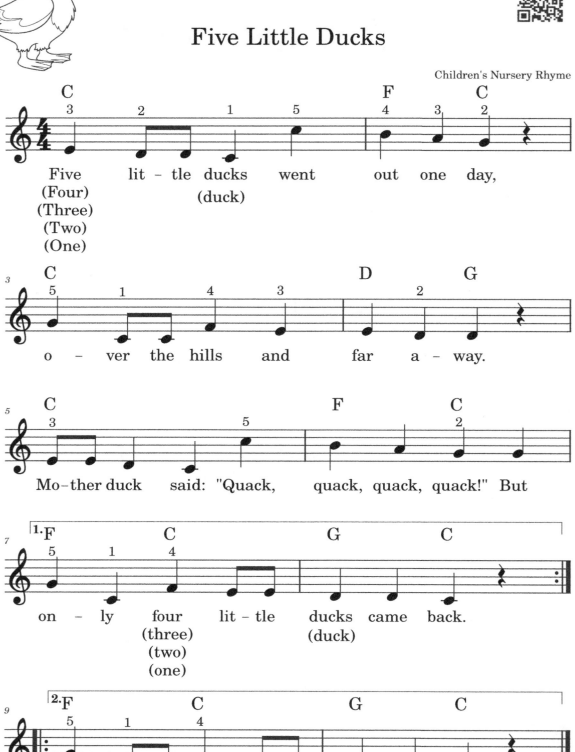

Five lit – tle ducks went out one day,
(Four) (duck)
(Three)
(Two)
(One)

o – ver the hills and far a – way.

Mo–ther duck said: "Quack, quack, quack, quack!" But

on – ly four lit – tle ducks came back.
(three) (duck)
(two)
(one)

none of the five lit – tle ducks came back.

Three Blind Mice

Traditional Children's Song

If You're Happy

Traditional

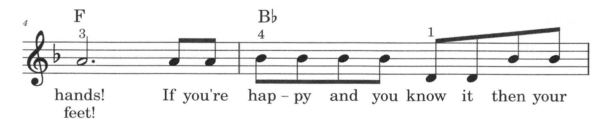

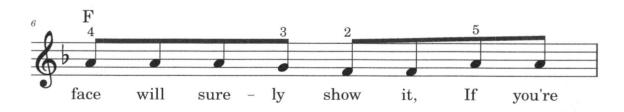

The Muffin Man

Traditional Nursery Rhyme

This Old Man

Welsh English Children's Counting and Marching Song

♩ = 120

This old man, he played one. He played knick-knack

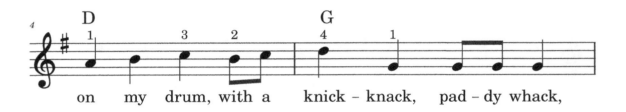

on my drum, with a knick – knack, pad – dy whack,

give the dog a bone! This old man came rol–ling home.

Hush! Little Baby

Traditional Americal Lullaby

Hush! Lit – tle ba – by, don't say a word,

Pa – pa's gon – na buy you a mock – ing – bird. And

if that mock – ing – bird don't sing,

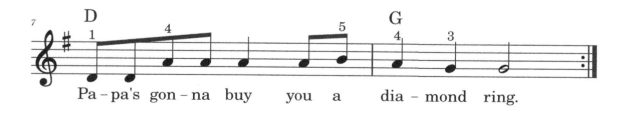

Pa – pa's gon – na buy you a dia – mond ring.

Deck the Halls

Traditional Christmas Tune

Deck the halls with boughs of hol - ly, fa-la-la-la-la - la - la-la-la! 'Tis the sea-son to be jol-ly, fa-la-la-la-la - la - la-la-la! Don we now our gay ap-pa-rel, fa-la-la - la-la-la - la-la-la! Troll the an-cient Yule-tide ca-rol, fa-la-la-la-la - la - la-la-la! See the bla-zing Yule be-fore us, fa-la-la - la-la-la - la - la - la! Troll the an - cient join the cho - rus, fa-la-la-la-la - la - la-la-la!

40

Oranges and Lemons

Traditional Nursery Rhyme

"Oran-ges and le – mons," say the bells of St. Cle-men's.

"You owe me five far things," say the bells of St. Mar-tin's.

"When will you pay me," says the bells of Old Bai-ley;

"When I grow rich," says the bells of shore ditch. "When will that

be – ?" says the bells of Step – ney–. "I do not know –," says the

great bell of Bow–. Here comes a can-dle to light you to

bed, and here comes a chop-per to chop off your head.

Sing a Song of Sixpence

Traditional Nursery Rhyme

Frere Jacques

Are You Sleeping?

Jean-Philippe Rameau

Fre – re Jac – ques, Fre – re Jac – ques,
Are you slee – ping, are you slee – ping,

dor – mez – vous? Dor – mez – vous?
Bro – ther John? Bro – ther John?

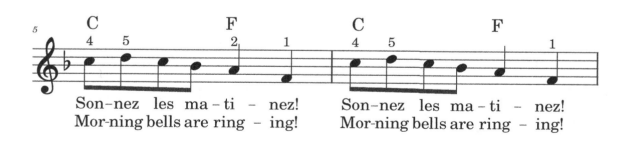

Son-nez les ma – ti – nez! Son-nez les ma – ti – nez!
Mor-ning bells are ring – ing! Mor-ning bells are ring – ing!

Ding, dang, dong! Ding, dang, dong!

Did You Ever See A Lassie

Traditional Nursery Rhyme

Did you   e – ver see a   las – sie,   a   las – sie,   a
lad – die   lad – die,

las – sie? Did you   e – ver see a   las-sie go   this way and
lad – die?   lad-die

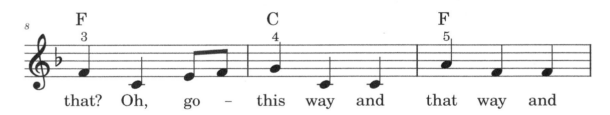

that? Oh,   go – this way and   that way and

this way and   that   way? Did you   e – ver see a

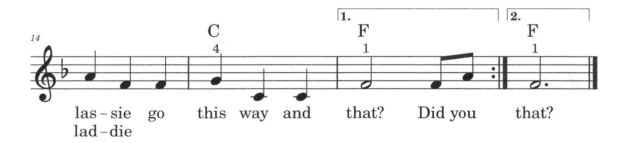

las – sie go   this way and   that? Did you   that?
lad – die

44

Jolly Old St. Nicholas

Traditional Christmas Carol

We Wish You A Merry Christmas

Traditional Christmas Carol

B. I. N. G. O.

Traditional Nursery Rhyme

There was a far – mer, had a dog, and

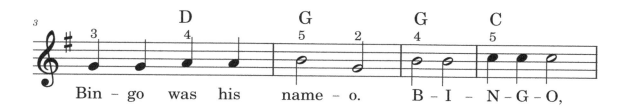

Bin – go was his name – o. B - I - N - G - O,

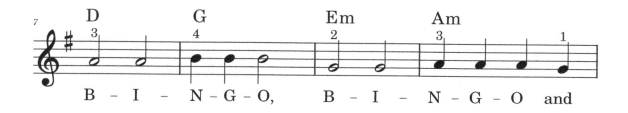

B - I - N - G - O, B - I - N - G - O and

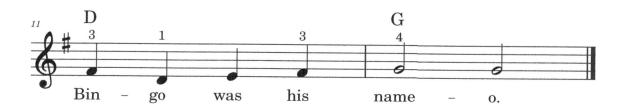

Bin – go was his name – o.

America

My Country 'Tis of Thee

transcribed by seyapianist

American Patriotic Hymn

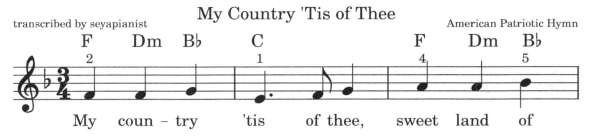

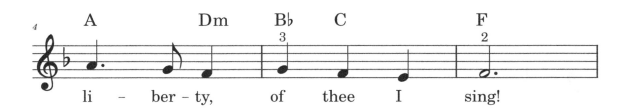

48

Pop Goes The Weasel

Traditional Nursery Rhyme

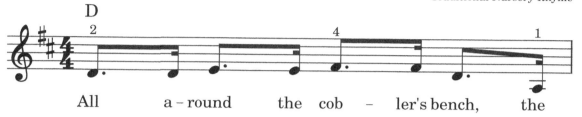

All a-round the cob - ler's bench, the

mon - key chased the wea - sel. The

mon - key thought t'was all in fun. Pop! Goes the wea - sel.

I've no time to wait or sigh, no pa-tience to wait 'till by and by

Kiss me quick, I'm off, good-bye, Pop! Goes the wea - sel.

Old MacDonald Had a Farm

Children's Nursery Rhymes

Level 3

MORE RESTS

You've already learned to recognize this rest:

Remember, it means you should wait and count to one before you play the next note.

This is a new rest symbol:

It is a shorter rest — take a break again, but this time, only wait half the time - as long as an 8th note.

MORE NOTATIONS

If you see two notes connected between them with a tie, like this:

That means you shouldn't stop and lift your finger between both notes, but rather you should play them immediately one after the other.

This symbol is called a natural. Remember when we learned about sharps and flats, and key signatures?

Well, a **natural** temporarily cancels out a key signature. In other words, if you have a specific note which is always played sharp, or flat, once you see it with this symbol you must remember to play it in its regular form.

This note looks funny but it's actually simple! It's played just how it looks – both notes at the same time. So, in this example, you'll play F and G together for the length of a half note.

O Christmas Tree

Traditional Christmas Hymn

O Christ-mas tree, O Christ-mas tree, how love-ly are your bran-ches! O Christ-mas tree, O Christ-mas tree, how love-ly are your bran-ches! Your boughs are green in sum-mer's glow and do not fade in win-ter's snow. O Christ-mas tree, O Christ-mas tree, how love-ly are your bran-ches!

Humpty Dumpty

transcribed by seyapianist

English Nursery Rhyme

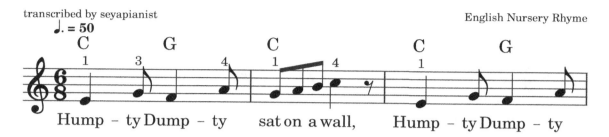

Hump – ty Dump – ty sat on a wall, Hump – ty Dump – ty

had a great fall, all the king's hor–ses and all the king's men

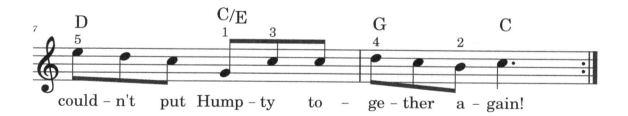

could – n't put Hump – ty to – ge – ther a – gain!

Hickory Dickory Dock

Traditional Nursery Rhyme

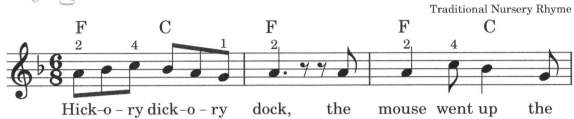

Hick–o – ry dick–o – ry   dock,   the   mouse went up   the

clock.   The   clock struck one,   the   mouse ran down,

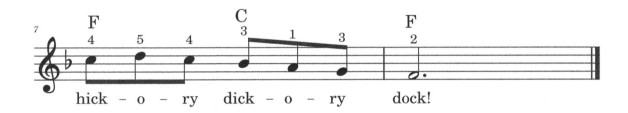

hick – o – ry   dick – o – ry   dock!

I Saw Three Ships

Traditional Christmas Carol

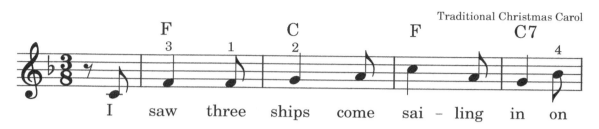

I saw three ships come sai - ling in on

Christ - mas day; on Christ - mas day. I

saw three ships come sai - ling in on

Christ - mas day, in the mor - ning.

When The Saints Go Marching In

Traditional Spiritual

Oh, when the saints go mar-ching in, oh, when the

saints go mar-ching in, O Lord I want to be in that

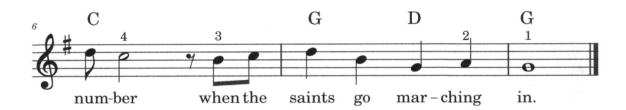

num-ber when the saints go mar-ching in.

Silent Night

Franz Gruber & Joseph Mohr

Amazing Grace

John Newton

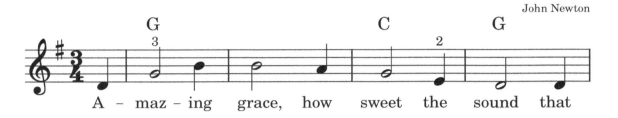

A - maz - ing   grace,   how   sweet   the   sound   that

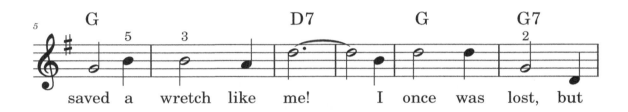

saved   a   wretch   like   me!   I   once   was   lost,   but

now   am   found,   was   blind   but   now   I   see.

The Farmer In The Dell

Traditional Nursery Rhyme

The far - mer in the dell, the

far - mer in the dell. Hey, ho, the

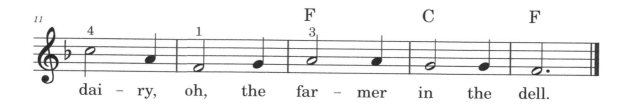

dai - ry, oh, the far - mer in the dell.

Row, Row, Row Your Boat

Children's Round

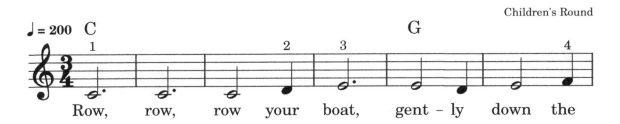

Row, row, row your boat, gent – ly down the

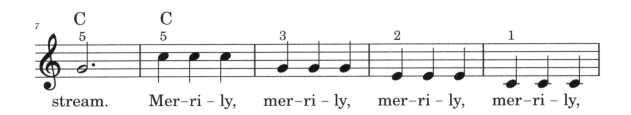

stream. Mer–ri – ly, mer–ri – ly, mer–ri – ly, mer–ri – ly,

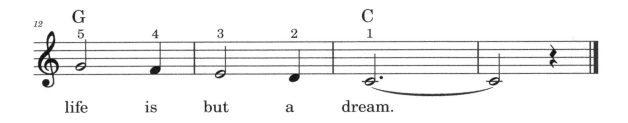

life is but a dream.

Hey Diddle Diddle

Traditional Nursery Rhyme

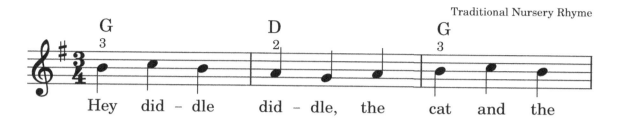

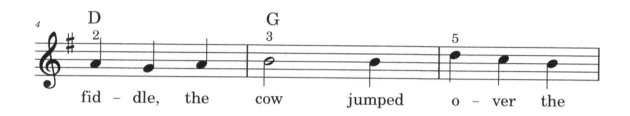

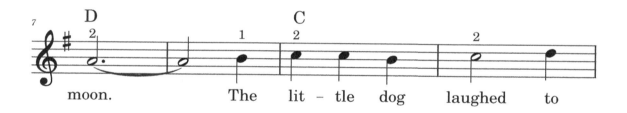

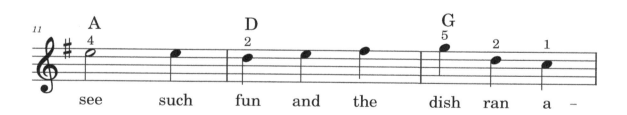

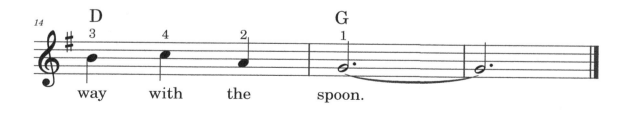

Little Miss Muffet

Traditional Nursery Rhyme

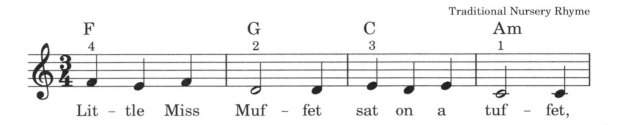

Lit – tle Miss Muf – fet sat on a tuf – fet,

ea – ting her curds and whey. A – long came a

spi – der who sat down be – side her and

frigh – tened Miss Muf – fet a – way.

Rock-a-bye Baby

Traditional Lullaby

Take Me Out To The Ball Game

Jack Norworth & Albert von Tilzer

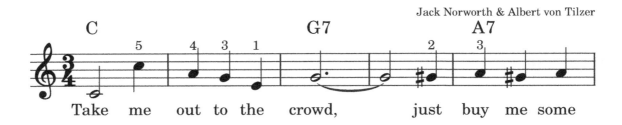

Take me out to the crowd, just buy me some

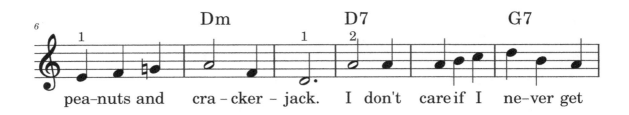

pea-nuts and cra - cker - jack. I don't care if I ne-ver get

back. Let me root, root, root for the home team, if

they don't win, it's a shame. For it's one, two,

three strikes, you're out, at the old ball game!

For S/he's A Jolly Good Fellow

Popular Song of Congratulations

For s/he's a jol – ly good fel – low, for s/he's a

jol – ly good fel – low, for s/he's a jol – ly good fel –

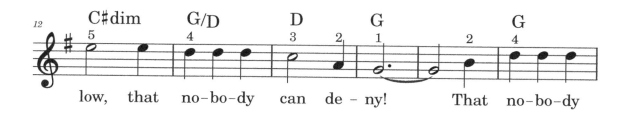

low, that no–bo–dy can de – ny! That no–bo–dy

can de – ny! That no–bo–dy can de – ny! For s/he's a

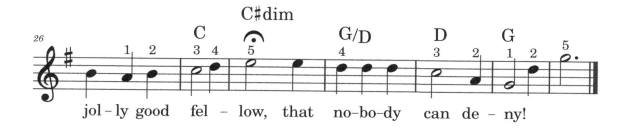

jol – ly good fel – low, that no–bo–dy can de – ny!

Happy Birthday

Traditional American Birthday Song

Hap-py   birth-day to   you, hap-py   birth-day to   you! Hap-py

birth-day, hap-py   birth-day, hap-py   birth-day to   you!

Jingle Bells

Traditional Christmas Carol

We hope you enjoyed this book and that it inspired in you a true love for music!

It would be so great if you could rate us on Amazon and leave a review, it means so much and helps us make more excellent content just like this.

APPENDIX A – CHORDS

Once you've learned to read and play notes with your right hand, you can go on to play with your left hand, too.

You'll notice that there are some capital letters above the music lines. These letters tell us what we should play with our left hand – and they are called chords.

Chords are a combination of three notes played at once, to accompany the melody being played with the right hand.

Chords are always played one octave lower than the melody!

PIANO CHORDS

KEY	MAJOR	MINOR	SEVENTH	AUGMENTED	DIMINISHED
A					
B					
C					
D					
E					
F					
G					

Made in the USA
Las Vegas, NV
04 November 2024

11094730R00044